# Matthew and Emma

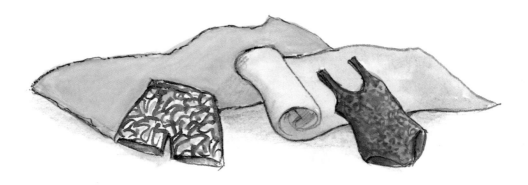

"Look at Matthew," said Emma.

"I am going down the slide," said Matthew.

"Here I come!"

"Look at Emma," said Matthew.

"Come on, Emma,"

said Dad.

"Look at Emma," said Matthew.

"I am going down the slide,"

said Emma.

"Here I come!"